NUCLEAR ENERGY
Amazing Atoms

Amy S. Hansen

PowerKiDS press™

New York

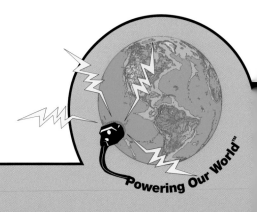

Powering Our World™

To my husband

Published in 2010 by The Rosen Publishing Group, Inc.
29 East 21st Street, New York, NY 10010

First Edition

Editor: Amelie von Zumbusch
Book Design: Greg Tucker
Photo Researcher: Jessica Gerweck

Photo Credits: Cover, pp. 5, 7 (inset), 13, 22 Shutterstock.com; p. 7 © www.iStockphoto.com/Mark Evans; p. 9 GSO Images/Getty Images; p. 11 Robert Francis/Getty Images; p. 15 Ron Case/Keystone/Getty Images; p. 17 Michael Melford/Getty Images; p. 19 Chuck Nacke/Time Life Pictures/Getty Images; p. 21 Mark Wilson/Getty Images.

Library of Congress Cataloging-in-Publication Data

Hansen, Amy.
  Nuclear energy : amazing atoms / Amy S. Hansen. — 1st ed.
      p. cm. — (Powering our world)
  Includes index.
  ISBN 978-1-4358-9328-3 (library binding) — ISBN 978-1-4358-9744-1 (pbk.) — ISBN 978-1-4358-9745-8 (6-pack)
  1. Nuclear energy—Juvenile literature. 2. Atoms—Juvenile literature. I. Title.
  TK9148.H36 2010
  621.48'3—dc22

                                2009023747

Manufactured in the United States of America

CPSIA Compliance Information: Batch #WW10PK: For Further Information contact Rosen Publishing, New York, New York at 1-800-237-9932

Contents

What holds your desk together? Your answer might be "screws," but that brings up still more questions. As all things are, screws are made of **atoms**. What holds atoms together? The nucleus, or center, of an atom is held together by something called the **nuclear force**. This force is strong. When something changes the nuclear force, atoms **release** lots of energy. This energy is called nuclear energy.

The Sun's light and heat are forms of nuclear energy. They are released by nuclear **reactions** in the Sun. On Earth, people capture nuclear energy by breaking **uranium** atoms apart. This reaction releases heat that we use to **generate** electricity.

4

Everything you can see when you look around is made of atoms. Even your body is made of atoms!

Atoms are too tiny to see, except with the best **microscopes**. However, atoms themselves are made up of even smaller things, called particles. These particles have energy. There are three kinds of particles, called protons, electrons, and neutrons. What kind of element an atom is depends on the number of protons it has. For example, gold always has 79 protons. Lead has 82 protons.

An atom's electrons circle around its nucleus. Protons and neutrons make up the nucleus. The protons and neutrons are held together by the nuclear force. Energy is released when these particles break apart or come together.

Diamonds are a form of the element carbon. *Inset:* Carbon atoms, such as the one in this drawing, have six protons.

7

The reaction that releases nuclear energy in the Sun is nuclear fusion. "Fusion" means "putting smaller things together to make something larger." In the Sun, two atoms of the element hydrogen fuse together to make one atom of the element helium. Hydrogen atoms have one proton, while helium atoms have two protons. This reaction releases lots of energy.

The nuclear force holding together an atom's nucleus is so strong that it is hard to form or break. Atoms do not usually fuse together. However, the Sun's center is very hot, and the **gravity** there is very strong. These conditions allow fusion to happen.

The temperature in the center of the Sun is about 27 million °F (15 million °C). This heat helps make fusion possible.

People can make electricity by causing a reaction called nuclear fission. "Fission" means "breaking apart." In nuclear fission, atoms are broken apart.

Scientists use certain uranium atoms for nuclear fission. Uranium atoms are very large. These big atoms break apart more easily than smaller ones would. Scientists break up a uranium atom with tiny neutrons. When a neutron hits the uranium atom, it breaks it into smaller atoms. This releases energy and frees other neutrons. The first neutron and the newly freed neutrons hit other uranium atoms. Those atoms break apart, too. Atoms continue to break apart and energy keeps being released.

People get the uranium used to generate nuclear power by digging it out of mines, such as this one in Australia.

Nuclear fission gives off heat energy. **Engineers** use a **nuclear reactor** to collect this heat and change it to electricity. The reactor holds uranium **pellets**. One pellet is about the size of your fingertip. It holds as much energy as 150 gallons (568 l) of oil. The pellets are put inside long metal rods and placed in the core. The core is a small room with thick, solid walls. It is filled with cold water.

Once the nuclear reaction starts, the rods send off heat. This warms up the water. The water is pumped to a **generator** that uses its heat to make electricity.

Nuclear plants are often near water. Nuclear fission makes more heat than can be used, so people often cool the plants with water.

Uranium is one of several elements whose atoms sometimes break apart naturally. Scientists noticed this over 100 years ago. They studied these elements and learned about the particles that make up atoms. For years, scientists tried to capture the energy that is released by uranium to make electricity.

After World War II started in 1939, many scientists tried to make bombs that used nuclear energy. In 1945, American scientists created the first nuclear bombs. The bombs helped end the war. Soon after, nuclear scientists started trying to make electricity again. The first American nuclear plant opened in 1957 in Shippingport, Pennsylvania.

The Calder Hall nuclear power station, in Cumbria, Great Britain, was the first big nuclear plant to supply power to businesses.

Unlike **fossil fuel** power plants, nuclear plants produce little air pollution. However, nuclear power is not perfect. Uranium must be dug out of the ground. This tears up land. Also, uranium is a nonrenewable energy source. This means that Earth's supply of uranium could get used up over time.

Another problem with nuclear power is nuclear waste. This is what is left over when uranium pellets will no longer work in a reactor. Nuclear waste leaks radiation, or energy that hurts living things. The waste must be stored carefully. However, it will leak radiation for about 100,000 years. No one knows if we can store nuclear waste safely for that long.

This nuclear waste was produced by California's Diablo Canyon Nuclear Power Plant. Such waste is carefully marked before being stored.

Engineers work hard to try to keep nuclear power safe, but two major **accidents** have happened. In 1979, engineers discovered that there was too little liquid in the core of the Three Mile Island nuclear power plant, near Middletown, Pennsylvania. Engineers put cool liquid in the cores of reactors so that they do not get too hot. The plant had to be shut down quickly.

In 1986, an even worse accident happened. Ukraine's Chernobyl reactor ran out of cooling liquid. The rods full of uranium pellets caught fire and melted the core. Many thousands of people got sick from the radiation.

After the accident at Chernobyl, people had to move out of the nearby towns. This man is measuring radiation in one of these towns.

By 2007, the United States had 66 nuclear power plants. The plants made a little less than a quarter of the electricity that Americans used that year. Other countries had another 340 nuclear power plants. Today, more are being built.

What will happen next? No one is sure. Some people say the problems that come with nuclear power are too big for us to use it. They worry about safety, both today and in the years to come. Other people support nuclear power because it produces little pollution. Many people like that it takes only a little uranium to make a lot of electricity. Nuclear power will likely be around for a long time.

These people are speaking out against the building of a nuclear waste storage space under Nevada's Yucca Mountain.

MOCK NUCLEAR WASTE CASK

STOP YUCCA MTN.

YUCCA MTN. DUMP: Tens of Thousands of Atomic Waste Trucks & Trains Through 43 States

21

Nuclear Energy Timeline

1789	Martin Heinrich Klaproth discovers uranium.
1896	Henri Becquerel discovers radiation in uranium.
1902	Ernest Rutherford and Frederick Soddy suggest how radioactivity works.
1934	Enrico Fermi breaks apart an atom and causes nuclear fission.
1942–1945	During World War II, the United States secretly builds an atomic bomb. The bomb works. The war ends.
1957	The first big nuclear power plant in the United States starts running in Pennsylvania.
1973	U.S. power companies start building 41 nuclear power plants, the most ever in one year.
1979	Three Mile Island nuclear power plant nearly has a partial **meltdown**. The accident brings safety changes.
1980	In the United States, more electricity is made from nuclear power than from oil for the first time.
1986	The Chernobyl nuclear power plant malfunctions. The core melts and radiation escapes.

Glossary

accidents (AK-seh-dents) Unexpected and sometimes bad things that happen.

atoms (A-temz) The smallest parts of elements.

engineers (en-juh-NEERZ) Masters at planning and building engines, machines, roads, and bridges.

fossil fuel (FO-sul FYOOL) Fuel, such as coal, natural gas, or gasoline, that is made from plants that died millions of years ago.

generate (JEH-neh-rayt) To make.

generator (JEH-neh-ray-tur) A machine that makes electricity.

gravity (GRA-vih-tee) The force that causes objects to move toward each other.

meltdown (MELT-down) When the core of a nuclear power plant gets too hot and lets harmful energy escape.

microscopes (MY-kruh-skohps) Instruments used to see very small things.

nuclear force (NOO-klee-ur FAWRS) The force that holds the centers of atoms together.

nuclear reactor (NOO-klee-ur ree-AK-tur) A machine in which nuclear power is safely created.

pellets (PEH-luts) Small, round things.

reactions (ree-AK-shunz) Actions caused by things that have happened.

release (ree-LEES) To let go.

uranium (yoo-RAY-nee-um) A heavy metallic element that gives off rays of energy.

Index

A
accident(s), 18, 22

C
center, 4, 8
core(s), 12, 18, 22

E
Earth, 4
electricity, 4, 10, 12, 14, 20, 22
electrons, 6
engineers, 12, 18

F
forms, 4

G
generator, 12
gravity, 8

H
heat, 4, 12

K
kinds, 6

L
light, 4

M
meltdown, 22
microscopes, 6

N
neutrons, 6, 10
nuclear reactor(s), 12, 16, 18
nucleus, 4, 6

P
particles, 6, 14
pellet(s), 12, 18
plant(s), 14, 16, 18, 20, 22
proton(s), 6, 8

R
reaction(s), 4, 8, 10, 12

S
Sun, 4, 8

Web Sites

Due to the changing nature of Internet links, PowerKids Press has developed an online list of Web sites related to the subject of this book. This site is updated regularly. Please use this link to access the list:
www.powerkidslinks.com/pow/nuclear/